MOSES
LEADER GUIDE

Moses:
In the Footsteps of the Reluctant Prophet

Moses
978-1-5018-0788-6 *Hardcover with jacket*
978-1-5018-0789-3 *e-Book*
978-1-5018-0790-9 *Large Print*

Moses: DVD
978-1-5018-0793-0

Moses: Leader Guide
978-1-5018-0791-6
978-1-5018-0792-3 *e-Book*

Moses: Youth Study Book
978-1-5018-0800-5
978-1-5018-0801-2 *e-Book*

Moses: Children's Leader Guide
978-1-5018-0802-9

Also by Adam Hamilton

24 Hours That Changed the World

Christianity and World Religions

Christianity's Family Tree

Confronting the Controversies

Creed

Enough

Final Words from the Cross

Forgiveness

Half Truths

John

Leading Beyond the Walls

Love to Stay

Making Sense of the Bible

Not a Silent Night

Revival

Seeing Gray in a World of Black and White

Selling Swimsuits in the Arctic

Speaking Well

The Call

The Journey

The Way

Unleashing the Word

When Christians Get It Wrong

Why?

For more information, visit www.AdamHamilton.org.

ADAM HAMILTON

MOSES

In the Footsteps of the
RELUCTANT PROPHET

Leader Guide
by Martha Bettis Gee

Abingdon Press / Nashville

Moses:
In the Footsteps of the Reluctant Prophet
Leader Guide

This book is printed on elemental chlorine-free paper.

978-1-5018-0791-6

17 18 19 20 21 22 23 24 25 26—10 9 8 7 6 5 4 3 2 1
MANUFACTURED IN THE UNITED STATES OF AMERICA

CONTENTS

TO THE LEADER

Welcome! In this study, you have the opportunity to help a group of learners explore the single most important figure in the Hebrew Bible—Moses. The study is based on Adam Hamilton's book and DVD, *Moses: In the Footsteps of the Reluctant Prophet*. Hamilton tells us that the story of Moses' life is the defining story of the Jewish people. Further, for Christians, Moses' life serves as the backdrop for much that is found in the Gospels. Throughout history, this story has continued to speak to each successive generation.

In the introduction to the book, Adam Hamilton observes that among the many things he appreciates about Moses' story is what an unlikely hero Moses was. But this book is not intended to be a biography of Moses, a verse-by-verse exposition of his story, or a scholarly commentary on Moses. Instead, Hamilton's hope is that the book will help readers not only come to know Moses, but to see how his life and story speak to our lives and stories today. His goal is that Moses' story will reveal something to us about God, about ourselves, and about God's will for our lives.

Scripture tells us that where two or three are gathered together, we can be assured of the presence of the Holy Spirit, working in and through all those gathered. As you prepare to lead, pray for that presence and expect that you will experience it.

The study includes six sessions, and it makes use of the following components:

- the book *Moses: In the Footsteps of the Reluctant Prophet*, by Adam Hamilton;
- the DVD that accompanies the study;
- this Leader Guide.

Participants in the study will also need Bibles, as well as either a spiral-bound notebook for a journal or an electronic means of journaling, such as a tablet. If possible, notify those interested in the study in advance of the first session. Make arrangements for them to get copies of the book so that they can read the introduction and chapter 1 before the first group meeting.

Using This Guide with Your Group

Because no two groups are alike, this guide has been designed to give you flexibility and choice in tailoring the sessions for your group. The session format is listed below. You may choose any or all of the activities, adapting them as you wish to meet the schedule and needs of your particular group.

The leader guide offers a basic session plan designed to be completed in a session about forty-five minutes in length. Besides the basic session plan, you will find additional activities that are optional. You may decide to add these activities or to substitute them for those suggested in the basic plan. Select ahead of time which activities the group will do, for how long, and in what order. Depending on which activities you select, there may be special preparation needed. The leader is alerted in the session plan when advance preparation is needed.

Session Format

Planning the Session

Session Goals
Scriptural Foundation
Special Preparation

Getting Started

> Opening Activity
> Opening Prayer

Learning Together

> Video Study and Discussion
> Book and Bible Study and Discussion
> More Activities (Optional)

Wrapping Up

> Closing Activity
> Closing Prayer

Helpful Hints

Preparing for the Session

- Pray for the leading of the Holy Spirit as you prepare for the study. Pray for discernment for yourself and for each member of the study group.
- Before each session, familiarize yourself with the content. Read the book chapter again.
- Choose the session elements you will use during the group session, including the specific discussion questions you plan to cover. Be prepared, however, to adjust the session as group members interact and as questions arise. Prepare carefully, but allow space for the Holy Spirit to move in and through the group members and through you as facilitator.
- Prepare the room where the group will meet so that the space will enhance the learning process. Ideally, group members should be seated around a table or in a circle so that all can see each other. Movable chairs are best because the group will often be forming pairs or small groups for discussion.
- Bring a supply of Bibles for those who forget to bring their own. Also bring writing paper and pens for those participants who do not bring a journal or a tablet or other electronic means of journaling.

- For most sessions you will also need a chalkboard and chalk, a whiteboard and markers, or an easel with large sheets of paper and markers.

Shaping the Learning Environment

- Begin and end on time.
- Create a climate of openness, encouraging group members to participate as they feel comfortable.
- Remember that some people will jump right in with answers and comments, while others need time to process what is being discussed.
- If you notice that some group members seem never to be able to enter the conversation, ask them if they have thoughts to share. Give everyone a chance to talk, but keep the conversation moving. Moderate to prevent a few individuals from doing all the talking.
- Communicate the importance of group discussions and group exercises.
- If no one answers at first during discussions, do not be afraid of silence. Count silently to ten, then say something such as, "Would anyone like to go first?" If no one responds, venture an answer yourself and ask for comments.
- Model openness as you share with the group. Group members will follow your example. If you limit your sharing to a surface level, others will follow suit.
- Encourage multiple answers or responses before moving on.
- To help continue a discussion and give it greater depth, ask, "Why?" or "Why do you believe that?" or "Can you say more about that?"
- Affirm others' responses with comments such as "Great" or "Thanks" or "Good insight," especially if it's the first time someone has spoken during the group session.
- Monitor your own contributions. If you are doing most of the talking, back off so that you do not train the group to listen rather than speak up.

- Remember that you do not have all the answers. Your job is to keep the discussion going and encourage participation.

Managing the Session

- Honor the time schedule. If a session is running longer than expected, get consensus from the group before continuing beyond the agreed-upon ending time.
- Involve group members in various aspects of the group session, such as saying prayers or reading Scripture.
- Note that the session guides sometimes call for breaking into smaller groups or pairs. This gives everyone a chance to speak and participate fully. Mix up the groups; don't let the same people pair up for every activity.
- As always in discussions that may involve personal sharing, confidentiality is essential. Group members should never pass along stories that have been shared in the group. Remind the group members at each session: confidentiality is crucial to the success of this study.

1.

THE BIRTH OF MOSES

Planning the Session

Session Goals

As a result of conversations and activities connected with this session, group members should begin to:

- explore fear, courage, and trust in stories of Moses' birth;
- examine examples of courageous and unexpected responses;
- encounter examples of how God works in the world through people;
- reflect on ways in which they might respond to God's word as revealed in the stories of Moses' birth.

Scriptural Foundation

The two midwives respected God so they didn't obey the Egyptian king's order. Instead, they let the baby boys live.

(Exodus 1:17)

When she couldn't hide him any longer, she took a reed basket and sealed it up with black tar. She put the child in the basket and set the basket among the reeds at the riverbank.

(Exodus 2:3)

Special Preparation

- For the opening activity, print the following at the top of four columns on a large sheet of paper or a board: who, when, where, and how.
- Have available a notebook or paper and pen or pencil for anyone who did not bring a notebook or an electronic device for journaling.
- Participants who have attended Sunday school and church since childhood are likely quite familiar with the story of Joseph that is the foundation for the story of Moses. Others who are new to the church may only have a sketchy familiarity with stories such as Joseph's famous coat. As you do a quick review of the Joseph narrative, be alert to those who may have a less extensive understanding, expanding on the highlights as necessary. The synopsis of the musical *Joseph and the Amazing Technicolor Dreamcoat* on Wikipedia can also give a quick overview.
- Decide if you will do any of the optional activities. For the activity in which participants place themselves in the biblical stories, print the following names on index cards: Pharaoh, Shiphrah, Puah, Moses' father, Moses' mother, Moses' sister, Pharaoh's daughter. Make enough cards that each participant can have one.
- For the activity about walking in the footsteps of Moses, a map of ancient Egypt will be helpful. If one is not available, use the maps in the chapter to sketch a simple outline map on a large sheet of paper. You will also need self-stick notes (or index cards and tape) and pens.
- For the activity on unexpected ways to stand against evil, arrange to show the short YouTube video White Flour, based on David LaMotte's book (https://www.youtube.com /watch?v=05etFVZasyg). If participants will be generating

a list of ways to support vulnerable children, check with your pastor or a member of your mission or outreach committee to find out if there are already initiatives underway by your congregation to support children and families.

Getting Started

Opening Activity

As participants arrive, welcome them to the study. Gather together. If participants are not familiar with one another, provide nametags and make introductions.

Call attention to the words on the posted sheet or board. Point out that these words are shorthand for some of the questions journalists seek to answer in their stories, and flesh out what each question is asking in terms of the biblical character, Moses:

- *Who* was Moses? Was he a real historical figure?
- *When* did he live?
- *Where* did the narrative about Moses take place?
- *How* do scholars believe the stories of Moses came to be recorded?

Depending on the size of your group, form pairs or small groups, and assign one of the question words to each. Invite participants to review the material in the introduction (or read it, if they have not yet had the opportunity to do so) and be prepared to report on differing views of scholars, as well as what view Adam Hamilton suggests on each question.

After allowing a few minutes for pairs or groups to work, ask each to report back to the large group. Invite any comments, observations, or questions about what the answers to the questions reveal about Moses. Point out that placing Moses and his story in context will help participants engage more fully in the study to come.

To the question of *why*, point out that Hamilton's intention in writing this book about Moses was not merely to summarize Moses' story, but to see what the story teaches us about ourselves, about humankind, and about God.

Opening Prayer

Pray together, using the following prayer or one of your own choosing.

We come, O Holy One of Israel, to explore Moses, the most significant figure of the Old Testament. Guide us as together we experience the power of ancient tales shared by firelight and later recorded and preserved. Most of all, grant that we may encounter you and your story in the story of Moses, that we may gain new insights about ourselves and about our place in that story. In the name of Jesus Christ we pray. Amen.

Learning Together

Video Study and Discussion

In this series, Adam Hamilton travels to Egypt and shows us the sites where Moses' story took place. In Session 1 we view awe-inspiring pyramids at Giza and temples at Thebes that show vividly the power of the Egyptian state that Moses would have to overcome. At the Nile River we learn how as a baby of slaves, Moses was found by Pharaoh's daughter and adopted.

- Learning about the pyramids and temples, what was as you had expected? What, if anything, was different or surprising?
- Why do you think Hamilton spends so much time talking about pyramids and temples?
- How does the information in today's video relate to Moses' story? to God's story?

Book and Bible Study and Discussion

Review Joseph's Story

Point out that the backdrop for the story of Moses is the story of Joseph. On a board or large sheet of paper, print the names Abraham and Sarah, Isaac and Rebecca. Point out that Jacob was one of two sons of Isaac and Rebecca and that Joseph was one of his sons. To review the story, say that Joseph was his father's favorite, and he gave Joseph a special coat. Ask a volunteer to tell what happened next. Continue having volunteers add brief details to complete Joseph's story. Avoid getting bogged down in the finer

Print (handwritten margin note)

story in magazine (handwritten note)

incidents of the story; Joseph's narrative serves only as a foundation for what is to come.

Explore the Role of Fear

Tell participants that beginning in Exodus 1:8, we read that a new king arose over Egypt who did not know Joseph. Invite a volunteer to read aloud Exodus 1:8-14. Ask participants to review quickly the information in the chapter about Pharaoh's response to the increase in the Israelite population. Invite them to consider the author's question about what the oppression of the Israelites can tell us about ourselves. Discuss the following:

- What are some examples from history in which fear of minority populations has led the United States and other nations to oppress, dehumanize, and at times even kill them?
- When faced with such situations, how are Christians to respond?

Explore Courage in the Face of Fear

Ask someone to read aloud verses Exodus 1:15-22, and call the group's attention to the material about the two midwives, Shiphrah and Puah. Note that this is one of the first recorded instances of civil disobedience. Discuss some of the following:

- How does the author define "fear of the Lord"? How would you distinguish that fear from the kind of fear that motivated Pharaoh?
- Have you ever been faced with two competing moral claims? What did you do, and how did you decide which claim should take precedence?
- What risks did Shiphrah and Puah take? What might have been the personal cost to the two women of resisting evil, and how might the outcome have been different?
- The author poses a question: Are you willing to stand against the authorities if what they call you to do is immoral or unjust? Have you ever taken a stand that put you in some jeopardy? What was the result?

Explore Unexpected Responses to Fear

Ask for a show of hands for those in the group who remember the story of Moses in the basket. Point out that for many people the story is a familiar and beloved one that they remember from childhood. Invite the group to set aside their previous impressions of the story and to listen with new ears as a volunteer reads Exodus 2:1-9. Encourage them to focus on the following:

- the danger to the infant;
- the risks that Moses' mother, sister, and Pharaoh's daughter were taking;
- the unexpected way in which all three women were able to ensure the baby's safety.

Following the reading, invite participants to offer observations on the three points.

Examine the Ways God Works

Invite participants to quickly scan Exodus 1 and 2. Point out that God is not explicitly mentioned anywhere in these verses, yet it is clear that God was working in this story. Discuss:

- How does the author suggest that God usually works in our world? Has this been your experience? Why or why not?
- What would you say is the role of Christians in God's actions in the world? What might be some ways of making ourselves more sensitive and attentive to the nudging of the Holy Spirit?
- When heartbreaking circumstances occur, the response of some is to say, "Everything happens for a reason" or to suggest that God never gives us more than we can handle. How would you respond to these statements?

Reflect on Fear, Courage, and Trust

The story of Moses involves themes of fear, courage, and trust. Invite the group to give examples of each. Encourage them to reflect on those themes in writing in their journals, responding to one or more of the following:

- In my own life, I am fearful about _____.
- Despite my fear, I will seek to respond with courage to
  _____.
- A difficult or heartbreaking situation with which I am dealing is
  _____.
- I will seek to put my trust in God and in God's working
  through myself and others. I will commit to listening more
  fully for the Spirit's word by engaging in practices such as
  _____.

More Activities (Optional)

Place Yourself in the Story

Distribute the prepared index cards, one per participant. Review the stories of Shiphrah and Puah and then the story of Moses in the basket, then ask participants to imagine themselves to be the character on their assigned card. Following each story, invite volunteers to describe what emotions and thoughts they imagined their character experiencing. Did they feel fearful? What response did that fear evoke? Then discuss:

- What do you imagine determined how each character responded to a fearful or threatening situation?
- How do you think God was working? What do you think made some characters receptive and others resistant to the movement of the Spirit?
- Where do you see creative, unexpected solutions to threats being employed?

Walking in the Footsteps of Moses: Part 1

Review with participants the information in the introduction and chapter 1 in which the author refers to his travels in Egypt as he sought to walk in Moses' footsteps. Ask the group to identify significant landmarks or locations described in the introduction and chapter 1, and record each on a self-stick note. These locations might include the Nile River, the Nile River Delta, the Land of Goshen, Memphis, Giza, the Valley of the Kings, Ramesses, and Thebes. Place the notes at the appropriate location on the map or map sketch that you prepared before the session. Discuss:

- What do the pyramids and other monuments suggest to you about the power of the pharaoh?
- Why do you imagine that such a powerful ruler was so fearful of the Hebrews?

White Flour: *Creative Civil Disobedience*

Remind the group that in Moses' story, individuals responded to a serious threat by resisting it, even in the face of fear. The midwives, Moses' family, and Pharaoh's daughter all responded in creative and unexpected ways.

Show the YouTube clip *White Flour*, the story of another creative act of civil disobedience, this one at a KKK rally. Discuss together the effectiveness of this response to racism. Ask:

- What risks were involved for the protestors?
- What was the response to their actions? How effective were they?

Explore Ways to Support Vulnerable Children

In reflecting on the story of Moses' adoption by Pharaoh's daughter, participants might consider whether God may be calling them to a ministry of adoption or offering foster care for a child in need of parents. Encourage them to give some thought and prayer to this possibility, but also suggest that there are many other ways to provide support and affirmation to vulnerable children. For example, if you have identified congregational initiatives in which to participate, point participants to contact persons. Then have them form pairs to brainstorm ways to support children, such as through mentoring or tutoring programs or big and little sister or brother programs. In the large group, compile a list of suggested programs and activities. Encourage participants to bring these ideas before God in their devotional times.

Wrapping Up

Point out that throughout Scripture, the words *fear not* or *be not afraid* are a continuing thread occurring many times. Read aloud Isaiah 43:1-3a, 4:

But now, says the LORD—
the one who created you, Jacob,
    the one who formed you, Israel:
Don't fear, for I have redeemed you;
    I have called you by name; you are mine.
When you pass through the waters, I will be with you;
    when through the rivers, they won't sweep over you.
When you walk through the fire, you won't be scorched
    and flame won't burn you.
I am the LORD your God,
    the holy one of Israel, your savior....
Because you are precious in my eyes,
    you are honored, and I love you.
    I give people in your place,
        and nations in exchange for your life.

Invite participants to reflect on this passage in the coming week, considering what risks and challenges they may be called to.

Remind the group to read chapter 2 before the next session.

Closing Activity

Invite participants to respond to the following:

- If it hadn't been for Shiphrah and Puah, _____.
- If it hadn't been for the actions of Moses' mother and sister, _____.
- If not for the action of Pharaoh's daughter, _____.

Encourage participants to reflect in the coming days on what creative acts of resistance, regardless of risk, they may be called to engage in.

Closing Prayer

O God, you call us to find ourselves in your story. Grant us the courage not to give in to fear and to find creative ways to resist what is wrong. Help us to trust that you can work in and through us to accomplish your purposes. Move us to compassion for those in need, and stir our will to be a part of your saving story. In the name of Jesus Christ we pray. Amen.

2.

TWO MOMENTS THAT DEFINED THE MAN

Planning the Session

Session Goals

As a result of conversations and activities connected with this session, group members should begin to:

- explore two defining moments in the life of Moses;
- examine how God may be at work in the wilderness experiences of our lives;
- consider how God can use the most reluctant and unlikely persons;
- reflect on ways in which they might respond to God's word as revealed in the bush that was burning and not consumed.

Scriptural Foundation

One day after Moses had become an adult, he went out among his people and he saw their forced labor. He saw an Egyptian beating a Hebrew, one of his own people. He looked around to make sure no one else was there. Then he killed the Egyptian and hid him in the sand.

(Exodus 2:11-12)

Moses said to God, "Who am I to go to Pharaoh and to bring the Israelites out of Egypt?"

(Exodus 3:11)

Special Preparation

- Provide journaling materials for anyone who did not bring a journal.
- Decide if you will do any of the optional activities. For the activity about walking in the footsteps of Moses, you will again need a map of the ancient world or a simple outline map sketched on a large sheet of paper. You will also need self-stick notes (or index cards and tape) and pens.
- For the dialogue between Moses and God at the burning bush, recruit two volunteers, preferably in advance of the session. Assign one the role of Moses and the other the role of God. If possible, point them to a version of the Bible in the vernacular, such as *The Message: The Bible in Contemporary Language*. To identify holy ground, cut sheets of red, yellow, and orange construction paper into a simple flame shape. You will also need markers, glue, or tape and a sheet of posterboard.
- For praying the newspaper, gather copies of recent newspapers or download and print copies of Internet news accounts.
- Obtain the hymn "Here I Am, Lord" and arrange for the group to sing it or recite the words together. Post the words for the group to see and refer to.

Getting Started

Opening Activity

As participants arrive, welcome them. If there are newcomers who were not present for the first session, invite a volunteer or two to quickly summarize the learnings from that session.

Form pairs, and invite participants to discuss the following with their partner:

- Have you ever been asked to take on a task you were reluctant to do?
- What was the reason for your reluctance? How did you respond? Did you decline the request? Make excuses? Or did you accept, albeit with reservations?

In the large group, ask a volunteer or two to describe what was discussed in the pairs. Then ask:

- In retrospect, do you think the invitation to take on the task might have been God's call? Why or why not?

Tell the group that in this session, they will explore two defining moments in the life of Moses.

Opening Prayer

Pray together, using the following prayer or one of your own choosing.

Open our eyes, O Holy One, to signs of your presence among us. Make us aware of what you are calling us to, and open our hearts this day to respond. In the name of your Son, Jesus Christ, we pray. Amen.

Learning Together

Video Study and Discussion

In Session 2 we follow Moses' exile from Egypt's royal household across the Sinai Desert to the Land of Midian, where he married and became a humble shepherd. We see him at the burning bush, where God called him to return to Egypt and free the Israelites from slavery.

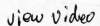

- What are some of the feelings Moses might have experienced in going from the royal family in Egypt to a humble shepherd in a desert wilderness?
- Moses encountered God in a burning bush. At what times in your own life do you feel that you have encountered God?

Book and Bible Study and Discussion

Explore Moses in Midian

Ask participants to quickly read Exodus 2:11-23, as well as the author's account of what happened when Moses went out to observe the forced labor of his people, the Israelites. Discuss the following: *Book ps. 44*

- The story of Moses killing the Egyptian taskmaster and the account of Moses at the well in Midian suggest that Moses had an intolerance for injustice, as well as compassion for those who were harassed or oppressed. These stories also point to the fact that he had the courage to act on behalf of those who were being mistreated. The author suggests that Moses' name may offer clues as to why he acted as he did. Why?
- Have you ever been bullied as a child or young person in school or as an adult in the workplace? How did you respond?
- The author suggests such treatment can make you bitter and resentful, or it can make you stronger and more compassionate. What do you think?

Examine Wilderness Experiences

ps 52

Hamilton speculates about how Moses, who had been raised in the court of Pharaoh, might have felt about the abrupt change in his fortune. He observes that Moses' time in the wilderness can serve in some ways as a metaphor for events in our own lives, those periods when things are not going well.

Remind the group that in the previous session, they explored the understanding that God's purposes are most often achieved through the actions of people. What are some ways that God can use our seasons in the wilderness to prepare and shape us for God's good purposes? Discuss:

26

ps54

- What skills must Moses have learned in his first years in Pharaoh's court? What skills must he have learned in his years in Midian as a shepherd?
- As you look back, are there times of the "wilderness" in your own life that have prepared you for later experiences? If so, in what ways were you prepared? What did you learn?

Explore the Encounter in the Burning Bush   *Look through* *God say*
Ex 3 & 4 *moses respond*

Form two groups. Ask one group to read through Moses' encounter with God at the burning bush in Exodus 3 and 4 and look for what God had to say to Moses. Ask the other group to look for the ways Moses responded to God.

After allowing a few minutes for the groups to work, come together in the large group. Work your way through the passage, eliciting what God ✗ had to say and how Moses responded each time. Then invite participants to name each excuse Moses made. Revisit the opening activity, inviting participants to consider what excuses they may have made for not → *what* undertaking a particular task. Discuss: *excuses*

our *excuses*

Make list then questions

- As you evaluate Moses' excuses to God, which ones seem valid? Think about excuses you have made. Which excuses came out of real feelings of inadequacy? Why were you reluctant to respond? *white paper*
- Think about how the Holy One responded to Moses. What do God's responses say about God? Do you sense patience? persistence? something else? *love - caring* *moses & excuse God's Resp*
- Who offered help to Moses in responding to God's challenging call? As Christians, what partners are available to us when we answer challenging calls today?

Reflect on Ways to Discern the Spirit's Call

Remind the group that frequently God does not send angels or engage in miraculous interventions in order to work in the world—God works through people—often unlikely people.

Invite a volunteer to read aloud Exodus 3:1-3. Ask: - *Read*

- What was unusual about the burning bush? Why do you think this unusual quality was significant?

Point out that Moses, or anyone else, might have responded to the burning bush by simply continuing to tend the sheep. Instead, Moses noticed that the bush was not consumed by the fire. And it was only after Moses took notice that the angel of the Lord appeared to him. Discuss:

- What are some ways we can cultivate more awareness of the "burning bushes" in our day-to-day lives?

For Hamilton, God's call less often comes in a dramatic burning-bush experience. Most often it comes as a feeling, nudge, or a compulsion that he can't shake. Discuss:

- What are some examples from your own life of God's nudgings? What are some practices that will enable us to be more responsive to them?

On a large sheet of paper or a board, record suggestions participants have of spiritual practices, as well as ways to discern God's call through attentiveness to the suffering of the world. Invite participants to respond to the following in their journals:

- In the coming week, I will commit to the following ways to culti-vate awareness of God's nudges: _____.

More Activities (Optional)

Walking in the Footsteps of Moses: Part 2

Ask participants to refer to places in chapter 2 where the author describes his travels in Egypt as he sought to walk in Moses' footsteps. Encourage them to read the descriptions and study the photos of places such as St. Catherine's Monastery. Ask them to identify significant landmarks or locations, and record each on a self-stick note. These additional locations might include St. Catherine's Monastery, Midian, and Avaris.

Place the notes at the appropriate location on the map you prepared. Discuss:

- How important is it to you whether or not the traditional sites of the burning bush or the well where Moses came to the aid of the women are actually the precise locations of these landmarks?

Do you think it would diminish how you would experience the traditional site? Why or why not?

- One of the interesting items on display in St. Catherine's Monastery is a copy of a letter said to have been dictated by Muhammad that granted protection not only for the monastery but for Christians. What, if any, are the implications of this action today in our own interfaith context?

A Dialogue between God and Moses

Invite the volunteers you recruited to present the dialogue between God and Moses. Afterward invite the group to discuss the encounter and the meaning in their own lives of the burning bush.

Identify Holy Ground

God told Moses to take off his sandals, for he was on holy ground. In ancient cultures and in many places today, it is a sign of respect for people to take off their shoes when entering another's home or a place of worship. Most of us would probably identify our places of worship as holy ground, but there are other holy places as well. Encourage participants to think of places or past experiences they might also identify as holy—places or persons or times when they have had a profound sense of God's presence and perhaps of God's call.

Distribute the flame shapes and markers. Invite participants to print a word or phrase identifying what is holy ground for them, and ask them to attach the flame to the poster. Discuss:

- Moses showed respect for God at the burning bush by removing his sandals. In what ways do you indicate your respect for God's presence in what you have identified as holy ground? Has your experience of holy ground translated into some action, or into a change of attitude or perception?

Pray the Newspaper

Hamilton writes that sometimes he discerns God's nudging as he's watching the news and seeing stories of pain and suffering. Distribute copies of newspapers or news accounts. Invite participants to breathe deeply in and out several times, settling into stillness and inviting the Spirit to be present. Allow several minutes for participants to scan news accounts in silence, asking God to guide them as they seek to discern what God might be calling them to do.

After allowing time for reading and meditating on the issues raised, close with a brief prayer. Encourage the group to pray the newspaper, Internet news, or televised news programs on a regular basis as a way of making themselves more attentive to God's call.

Wrapping Up

Invite the group to reflect on the two defining moments in Moses' life that they have explored in this session. Ask them to consider one or both of the following statements. Read each statement, inviting volunteers to respond out loud with a word or phrase.

- Like Moses, who had to flee to Midian after murdering the Egyptian, I have had experiences of being in the wilderness. Looking back, I can say I learned_____.
- Like Moses, I have known times when I was reluctant to accept a call from God. I felt ill prepared, but_____.

Remind the group to read chapter 3 before the next session.

Closing Activity

Call the attention of the group to the words of the posted hymn "Here I Am." Point out that the hymn's refrain reflects how Moses responded to God's call in the burning bush. Sing or recite the first stanza of the hymn, using that refrain.

Closing Prayer

God of the burning bush, we sometimes don't feel up to answering your call. We lack the skills or the vision or the will to do what needs to be done. Yet we know that you persist. Grant that when we hear you calling, "Get going! I'm sending you!" we may respond: "Here I am, Lord, send me!" Amen.

3.

THE EXODUS

Planning the Session

Session Goals

As a result of conversations and activities connected with this session, group members should begin to:

- explore the role of Moses, an unlikely prophet, in participating in God's redemptive act of the Exodus;
- examine the plagues God visited on Egypt;
- encounter parallels to our own redemption story and how we make that story our own;
- reflect on ways in which we might respond to God's word as revealed in the story of the Exodus.

Scriptural Foundation

The LORD said to Moses in Midian, "Go back to Egypt because everyone there who wanted to kill you has died." So Moses took his wife and his children, put them on a donkey, and went back to the land of Egypt.

(Exodus 4:19-20)

The LORD replied to Moses, "Now you will see what I'll do to Pharaoh. In fact, he'll be so eager to let them go that he'll drive them out of his land by force."

(Exodus 6:1)

Special Preparation

- Continue to provide journaling materials for those who did not bring any.
- It would be tempting to take the entire session to explore intriguing ways to view the plagues. Encourage participants instead to place that information in the larger context of the salvation story of how God worked in and through the events of the Exodus.
- On a large sheet of paper or a board, prepare a storyboard outline for the opening activity. At the top of the board or paper, print: "Pharaoh oppressed the Israelites with forced labor." At the bottom, print: "With his father-in-law's blessing, Moses got his wife and family and returned to Egypt."
- For the activity examining the ten plagues, print the following on a large sheet of paper or a board to use as a reference: First plague: Exodus 7:1-25; Second: Exodus 8:1-15; Third: Exodus 8:16-19; Fourth: Exodus 8:20-32; Fifth: Exodus 9:1-7; Sixth: Exodus 9:8-12; Seventh: Exodus 9:13-35; Eighth: Exodus 10:1-20; Ninth: Exodus 10:21-29; Tenth: Exodus 11:1-10; 12:29-30.
- Decide if you will do any of the optional activities. For all three optional activities, it will be helpful to have access to smartphones or reference books. For the activity on the Seder, arrange to download the YouTube clips and arrange for showing them. For the activity about walking in Moses' footsteps, you will again need a large map or an outline sketch on large paper and self-stick notes (or index cards and tape).
- Obtain the closing hymn, "How Firm a Foundation" and arrange for accompaniment.

Getting Started

Opening Activity

As participants arrive, welcome them.

Gather together. Say that before going forward with the story of Moses, it is helpful to review what has already happened. Remind participants that often in a television series that has had several episodes, a new episode will be prefaced by a short segment that brings viewers up to speed on what has happened in previous episodes. Invite the group to imagine they are creating an outline or a storyboard for such an update. Ask them to call out major events that might be in a segment called "Previously on 'Moses: Unlikely Prophet,'" and jot those events down quickly on the prepared storyboard outline.

With this review in mind, the group is ready to encounter the story of the Exodus.

Opening Prayer

Pray together, using the following prayer or one of your own choosing.

Eternal God, we remember your enduring promise to be with us always. Be with us now as we continue our encounter with the story of Moses. Open our eyes to our own part in the continuing story of your loving way with humankind. In the name of Jesus we pray. Amen.

Learning Together

Video Study and Discussion

In Session 3 we follow Moses back to Egypt and learn of his struggles with Pharaoh to free the Israelites from slavery. He leads them across the Reed Sea, where God defeats Egypt's deities and the world's most powerful army.

- Have you ever taken on a task that seemed especially difficult or even impossible? What was your experience, and how do you think it compared with Moses' experience?

- What were the ten plagues that God brought down on Egypt? Do you think they were natural or supernatural events? Why?

Book and Bible Study and Discussion

Explore the Plagues

Refer the group to the material in the text under the heading "Pharaoh of the Exodus." Ask a volunteer or two to describe what archaeology tells us about Ramesses II, and invite the group to look over the photos included in the chapter. Then ask the group to imagine the face-off of Moses and Aaron with Pharaoh to be something like a boxing match. Discuss:

[handwritten: p.74]

[handwritten: So desert 3 days]

- Describe the first interchange between Pharaoh and Moses and Aaron. What were the brothers asking for? What was Pharaoh's response to them, and how did Pharaoh up the ante? *[handwritten: more bricks]*
- How did God respond? *[handwritten: plagues]*

Recall for participants that in the book's introduction, they explored three ways of approaching Scripture:

- the *maximalist approach*, in which the biblical accounts from Abraham to Solomon are viewed as either largely or entirely historical and historically accurate;
- the *minimalist approach*, which asserts that stories of Moses and the Exodus are not dependent upon the story being historical, any more than Homer's *Iliad* or *Odyssey* are dependent upon whether Achilles or Odysseus were real people;
- a position *in between* that holds that the authors and editors of the Torah were writing about an actual historical figure named Moses, but the story is more like a film "based upon actual events" than a documentary.

Note that we might view the plagues literally as a maximalist would, or we might recognize that many of the plagues appear to be naturally occurring plagues that at times afflicted ancient Egypt (and are still seen from time to time today). Depending on the size of your group, form ten pairs or small groups and assign one plague to each, or simply assign one or two plagues per participant if your group is small.

Ask participants to quickly scan the material in the chapter about their plague, as well as the Scripture passage that relates what happened. After allowing a few minutes, ask each to report on how their assigned plague might be seen as a natural occurrence.

Hamilton reminds us that there is another way to look at the plagues: as a contest between the God of Israel and the whole pantheon of Egyptian gods and goddesses. Call the group's attention to the graphic in the chapter showing the ten plagues, as well as to what the author has to say about Egyptian gods. Discuss: *p. 83*

- Does it make a difference if we look at the plagues, not as a contest between Moses and Pharaoh, but as a cosmic battle between God and the gods of Egypt? If so, how? *yes*

Ask each person or pair to revisit the Scripture passage and read aloud the following verses (shown on the large sheet of paper or board you prepared before the session): First plague: Exodus 7:1-25; Second: Exodus 8:1-15; Third: Exodus 8:16-19; Fourth: Exodus 8:20-32; Fifth: Exodus 9:1-7; Sixth: Exodus 9:8-12; Seventh: Exodus 9:13-35; Eighth: Exodus 10:1-20; Ninth: Exodus 10:21-29; Tenth: Exodus 11:1-10; 12:29-30. Discuss:

- What two explanations does Hamilton suggest to explain the shift from Pharaoh hardening his heart to God hardening Pharaoh's heart? What seems plausible to you? *p. 90*
- Hamilton invites us to consider what he calls contemporary plagues, one of which he identifies as the Great Recession of 2008. What "god" would you say was revealed to hold allegiance in that crisis? What other gods seem to hold sway in our culture today? Are there other contemporary counterparts to plagues, or are there priorities ("gods") that have the potential of leading to a plague?

Call attention to Hamilton's comments, as well as maps and illustrations, about the location of the Reed Sea where the Israelites may have crossed and the kind of challenge they were up against in Pharaoh's army and chariots. Ask:

- What difference, if any, does it make that the Israelites may have made a crossing that was less dramatic than that traditionally portrayed in film? What if we view it, as Hamilton suggests, as more like a film "based upon actual events" than a documentary?
- How does it alter our understanding of the crossing if we focus less on details and more on the crossing as a contest of God against the greatest military force of the time?

Encounter Parallels to Our Own Redemption Story

Adam Hamilton quotes a rabbi friend about the Passover Seder: "This is our defining story. If you are a Jew, you've got to get this. It defines who we are as a people."

Form pairs, and invite participants to work together with their partner to identify parallels or areas of foreshadowing between the Passover story, the defining narrative of salvation for Jews, and the death and resurrection of Jesus Christ, the defining narrative of salvation for Christians.

After allowing a few minutes for pairs to work, invite volunteers to report what they found. Ask:

- What do you think grace has to do with the Exodus story? Where do we see grace in our own story?
- If you were asked to describe the defining story for Christians, what would you say? Could you articulate that story clearly, as devout Jews are able to describe the meaning of the Seder meal?

Reflect on Responding to God's Call

Despite Moses' reluctance to respond to God's call, the story of the Exodus reveals that God once again chose an unlikely prophet through whom to work redemption. Invite the group to name others in the story of Moses who were unlikely choices for pivotal roles, such as the midwives and Moses' mother and sister. Note that the author also lifts up Zipporah, Moses' wife.

Invite participants to revisit what happened following Moses' encounter at the burning bush. Ask someone to read aloud Exodus 4:27-31. Discuss:

- What was Aaron's role in this story? What was Moses' role? How did the two roles complement each other?

The author observes that nearly always when God calls us to do something, another person is called to come alongside us and help. He suggests that many of us will find ourselves in the role of Aaron at some point in our lives. Ask the group to brainstorm ways they might cultivate an awareness of opportunities to play a subordinate but nevertheless critical role such as Aaron's, whether at church or in the community. Then ask them to take a few moments to respond in their journals to the following:

- As I seek to discern God's call to be a part of the healing, redemptive work in the world, I will also try to be open to persons and situations where I can be someone else's Aaron, helping others pursue the calling God has placed on their lives. I will cultivate attentiveness to this call by _____.

More Activities (Optional)

Walking in the Footsteps of Moses: Part 3

Invite participants to find Tanis, Mount Sinai, and the possible location of the Reed Sea on the map, and mark these places with self-stick notes or index cards as in previous sessions. Also spend time examining the photographs in the chapter, as well as doing an online search for information about Ramesses II. One relevant site to explore is http://kingtutone.com/pharaohs/ramses2/.

Discuss what the information reveals about Ramesses' power and influence.

Research the Egyptian Gods

Form pairs and assign one of the plagues to each pair. Invite participants to do some online research about the Egyptian god that could be identified with their assigned plague. In the large group, have each pair report on their findings.

Explore the Seder

To learn more about the Seder meal, show participants two clips from the site JewFAQ.com: "Seder Part 1: The Seder Plate" and "Seder Part 2: Kaddeish, Urechatz, Karpas, Yachatz." The website Judaism 101 has additional information about the Seder meal.

Wrapping Up

Invite participants to respond to the following prompts about the Exodus story:

- In the story I am troubled by _____.
- I find comfort in _____.
- I still have questions about _____.

Invite the group to listen in silence as you read the following affirmations the author gives us in assessing the meaning of the Exodus story for Christians:

- God cares about the nobodies.
- God will ultimately defeat the arrogant, prideful, and cruel.
- God sees our suffering, and God will deliver us.
- We don't have to remain enslaved to the things that bind us.
- God can set us free.

Encourage the group to consider which of these affirmations they most relate to and what actions they may be called to take in response.

Closing Activity

Moses was able to depend not only on the support of Aaron but also on the assurance of God's abiding presence with him. Sing or recite together a closing hymn, "How Firm a Foundation."

Closing Prayer

God of the Exodus, we give thanks for your saving grace. Go with us now, as you have promised. Continue to abide with us, and by your Spirit make your presence known. Keep us ever more aware of how we may be a part of your redemption story. In the name of Jesus. Amen.

4.

THE TEN COMMANDMENTS

Planning the Session

Session Goals

As a result of conversations and activities connected with this session, group members should begin to:

- explore the Ten Commandments, God's basic ordering of society;
- examine how the commandments offer a vision for how we live, love, and relate to one another;
- encounter challenges the commandments place on us in our contemporary culture;
- reflect on ways in which group members might respond to God's word as revealed in the Ten Commandments.

Scriptural Foundation

The LORD called to [Moses] from the mountain, "This is what you should say to Jacob's household and declare to the Israelites: You saw what I did to the Egyptians, and how I lifted you up on eagles' wings and brought you to me. So now, if you faithfully obey me and stay true to my covenant, you will be my most precious possession out of all the peoples, since the whole earth belongs to me. You will be a kingdom of priests for me and a holy nation."

(Exodus 19:3b-6a)

Then God spoke all these words:

I am the LORD your God, who brought you out of the land of Egypt, out of the house of slavery; you shall have no other gods before me.

You shall not make for yourself an idol....

You shall not make wrongful use of the name of the LORD your God....

Remember the sabbath day, and keep it holy....

Honor your father and your mother....

You shall not murder.

You shall not commit adultery.

You shall not steal.

You shall not bear false witness against your neighbor.

You shall not covet....

(Exodus 20:1-17 NRSV)

Special Preparation

- Continue to make journaling materials available for those who did not bring any.
- Because chapter 4 deals exclusively with the Ten Commandments, this session devotes the bulk of the time to an in-depth examination of each commandment and its implications for faithful living. After spending a few minutes on the opening activity, plan to spend twenty-five minutes or so on the single exploration activity.

- If you decide that the suggested exploration activity is not the best choice for your group, look over the optional activities for other ways to explore the commandments. For the activity expanding the spirit of the commandments, you will need to cut sheets of paper or posterboard into shapes similar to that of your tabletops and provide markers as well as scratch paper. For the activity about walking in Moses' footsteps, you will again need a large map or an outline sketch on large paper and self-stick notes (or index cards and tape).

- For the closing activity, ask permission to borrow the pitcher, chalice, and plate used by your congregation in the sacrament of the Lord's Supper. Also plan to bring an uncut loaf of bread and some grape juice.

Getting Started

Opening Activity

Welcome participants as they arrive. Gather together. On a large sheet of paper or a board, print the words *wall* and *fence*. Invite participants to respond, popcorn style, with the first words or phrases that come to mind when reading these words. Continue eliciting responses as long as participants have them, and encourage a variety of responses. When responses slow, discuss the following:

- What is the function of a wall or a fence? Is it to keep something in, to keep something out, or both?
- Is a fence or a wall a positive thing, or is it negative? If it serves as a boundary, is that a good thing or a bad thing?

Tell participants that in today's session, they will be exploring the Ten Commandments, God's plan for ordering society. They will examine how these ten rules for living provide a boundary that delineates how we should relate to God and to others.

Opening Prayer

Pray together, using the following prayer or one of your own choosing.

God of Sinai, we are in awe of your power and might. Guide us today in our exploration, that we may be faithful and true to your covenant with us. For we ask it in Jesus' name. Amen.

Learning Together

Video Study and Discussion

In Session 4 we trace the journey of the Israelites as they left Egypt and set out into the desert. We learn about their complaints and God's responses. Finally we arrive at St. Catherine's Monastery at the foot of Mount Sinai and hike up the mountain where Mose received the Ten Commandments.

- Why do you think the Israelites complained so much after God had freed them from slavery? What did they learn? What do we learn from observing them?
- Why do you think Adam Hamilton felt it was so important to pray on his hike up Mount Sinai? If you had been there, what would you have prayed for?

Book and Bible Study and Discussion

Explore the Ten Commandments

Tell participants they will be assigned a commandment and given about ten minutes to explore it. They should read the information in the chapter on that commandment. On their sheet, they should print questions (perhaps including some the author poses) in one area and make comments or observations about the commandment in another. Depending on the size of your group, form ten pairs or small groups, or if your group is very small, ask people to work on their own.

When your allotted time for this activity has elapsed, invite individuals, pairs, or groups to take several minutes to move around the room, reading the comments and questions others have recorded about each commandment and adding other comments and questions that occur to them.

Gather together in the large group. Remind the group that the commandments, then as now, function as theological statements, as a vision for human living, and as moral and emotional "guardrails." Discuss:

- The commandments offer a vision of how we live, love, and relate to one another. How would you describe that vision?
- How would you describe the relationship between the Ten Commandments and the idea of covenant?

Invite participants to respond to the following:

- I see the commandments as helpful boundaries for living in that they_____.
- I have questions about _____.

Encounter Challenges and Reflect on Responses

Invite the group to look again at the information on the commandment they explored, noting in particular the questions posed by the author. Ask those who explored a particular commandment to name aspects of our contemporary culture that pose a challenge to us as we seek to be faithful to the commandments.

For example, in considering the first two commandments, the author invites us to ask ourselves what is of the highest importance in our lives. Is it our career? our friends? our family? How does society exert pressure to make these the driving forces in our lives? Invite the group to name other aspects of contemporary culture—for example, consumerism—that pose challenges to those seeking to be faithful, not just to the letter of the commandments but to the spirit of each law and of the sum total of the commandments. List these aspects on a large sheet of paper or a board.

Invite participants to choose one of the cultural aspects on the list that represents a particular challenge to them. Ask them to respond to the following by writing in their journals:

- In seeking to follow the _____ Commandment, I am challenged by_____. I commit to praying for discernment about how to live more faithfully.

More Activities (Optional)

Explore Commandments about God and Neighbor

The first four commandments order our relationship with God, while the remaining six order our relationship with one another. Having a right relationship with God is the foundation for a right relationship with others. Form two groups. Assign the first four commandments to one group and the remaining six to the other. Invite each group to examine their assigned commandments with the goal of answering the following:

- What do the commandments have to say about the relationship (for the first four commandments) of God to the people, and about the relationship (for the remaining six commandments) of the people to their neighbors?

Explore Parallels in the Gospel Story

There are many points at which Moses' story parallels the Gospel story, where the Gospel writers seemed to intend that their readers note allusions to the stories in Exodus. Invite the group to refer to the chapter for examples of this.

Create Expanded Tablets

Invite participants to consider the expanded commentary on the commandments that was offered by Jesus in the Sermon on the Mount (in Matthew 5). Ask them to imagine that someone posted tablets describing these expanded commandments. What words could or should be written on those tablets? For example, the tablet on the sixth commandment might include not just the words "You shall not kill" but also a discussion of the culture of violence in media that may fuel a devaluation of human life.

Assign a commandment to each individual, pair, or small group, depending on the size of your group. Give each of these a marker and the "tablets" you prepared before the session. Allow some time for participants to discuss what they might write and to prepare their tablets. Afterward, in the large group, ask groups to explain their tablets. Discuss:

- What difference might it make if our lawmakers took the implications of Jesus' expanded commandments seriously as they passed legislation?
- What difference might those implications make to merchants and business people? Or, to those developing and producing media and digital games?

Debate a Proverb

Form two groups, arbitrarily assigning one group the affirmative position and the other group the negative position on the following proverb: "Good fences make good neighbors." Ask each group to discuss how they would support their position by referring to the Ten Commandments as boundaries for behavior. Ask for a volunteer from each group to be the debater. Allow several minutes for preparation, then hold the debate, with the remaining members of both groups serving as the audience. Following the debate, debrief with the group.

Walking in the Footsteps of Moses: Part 4

Invite participants to locate the Sinai Peninsula, Jebel Musa (Mount Sinai), the St. Catherine's Monastery on the map, and mark them with self-stick notes or index cards as in previous sessions. Also spend time examining the photographs in the chapter. Refer the group to the author's description of God's awe-inspiring presence on the mountain, and encourage them to imagine such an encounter in light of the photographs shown in the chapter.

Wrapping Up

The Ten Commandments are sometimes referred to as the Ten Words. Ask the group to reflect in silence on the Ten Commandments and their meaning. Then ask them to call out one or two words that express their thoughts on each commandment.

Remind the group to read chapter 5 before the next session.

Closing Activity

Call the group's attention to Exodus 24:3-8, in which Moses gathers the people to commit to the Ten Commandments and the expanded body of Law. Point out that this passage makes reference to the blood of the covenant, an integral part of the ritual in which the people promise to be obedient.

Invite the group to consider the parallel between this ritual in Exodus and the words of institution of the Lord's Supper. Pour the juice into the chalice. Ask participants to reflect on the chalice, the plate, and the bread as you read the words of institution aloud from Luke 22:14-20.

Closing Prayer

O God, once we were no people, but now we are your people. We give thanks for your law that leads us into a right relationship with you and with our neighbor. Go with us now as we seek to live more faithfully. For we ask it in the name of Jesus Christ, who embodies the new covenant. Amen.

5.

LESSONS FROM THE WILDERNESS

Planning the Session

Session Goals

As a result of conversations and activities connected with this session, group members should begin to:

- explore lessons of shared leadership from Israel's time in the wilderness;
- examine the role of sacred spaces for the Israelites and for us;
- encounter the impact of complaining and fear;
- reflect on ways in which participants might respond to God's word as revealed in wilderness wanderings.

Scriptural Foundation

All the Israelites criticized Moses and Aaron. The entire community said to them, "If only we had died in the land of Egypt or if only we

47

had died in this desert! Why is the LORD bringing us to this land to fall by the sword? Our wives and our children will be taken by force. Wouldn't it be better for us to return to Egypt?" So they said to each other, "Let's pick a leader and let's go back to Egypt."

(Numbers 14:2-4)

Special Preparation

- Again provide journaling materials for those who did not bring a journal.
- Decide if you will do any of the optional activities. For exploring thin places, head three separate large sheets of paper with the following: Thin Places, Mountaintop Experiences, Shadow of Death Experiences. For the activity about walking in Moses' footsteps, you will again need a large map or an outline sketch on large paper and self-stick notes (or index cards and tape).

Decide if you would like to sing or recite the closing hymn suggested for this session, "Guide Me, O Thou Great Jehovah," or if you would prefer to sing or recite "How Firm a Foundation" again. In either case, obtain the hymn and arrange for accompaniment as needed.

Getting Started

Opening Activity

Welcome participants as they arrive. Gather together. Remind participants that in session 2, they considered Moses' experience in the wilderness following his murder of the Egyptian. Invite the group to think about what a wilderness is like. Form pairs, and ask participants to discuss the following with their partners:

- What constitutes a wilderness? For you, what is a wilderness is like?
- Think about a time in your life when you experienced wandering in the wilderness—not in the literal sense of hiking or camping in rugged, remote territory, but spiritually. What was the cause? Was it of your own making, or were there circumstances beyond your control?

- What were your emotions during that time? What challenges did you face? How did you get through it, and what did you learn?

In the large group, ask one or two volunteers to describe their wilderness experience. Note that the Israelites' wilderness wanderings represented a significant and transformative time in the life of God's people. Tell the group that in this session, they will explore wilderness time and in the process encounter several lessons that emerge from that experience.

Opening Prayer

Pray together, using the following prayer or one of your own choosing.

Eternal God, we have sometimes known times when we wondered if our wilderness wanderings would ever end. In those times, we have longed to break free from uncertainty, apprehension, and negativity. Guide us now as we seek to learn what you would have us to know about such times, that we may embrace your promises more fully. For we ask it in the name of Jesus Christ, who knew what it was to experience the loneliness and trials of the wilderness. Amen.

Learning Together

Video Study and Discussion

Session 5 describes the Israelites' years in the wilderness after leaving Egypt, including the feeding of the people, their complaints, and the building of the Tent of Meeting. The temples at Luxor and Karnak show how the structure of Egyptian temples was used as a model for the Tent of Meeting, culminating in the Holy of Holies.

- Have there been times in your life when you complained a lot? What did you learn from those experiences? What did you learn by reading about the Israelites' complaints?
- As a group, draw up a list of pros and cons for (a) the Israelites' life in Egypt and (b) their life in the desert.

Book and Bible Study and Discussion

Explore Lessons of Leadership

As the Israelites were camped near Mount Sinai, Moses' father-in-law Jethro, Midian's priest, came to see him. There Moses told Jethro the story of God's deliverance of the Israelites. After Jethro declared his affirmation of the Lord as the greatest of all the gods, he offered Moses some valuable advice. Ask a volunteer to read Exodus 18:13-27 aloud.

Remind the group that in previous sessions, they encountered the role of Aaron in providing support for his brother. In this session, our attention is directed to principles of shared leadership. Invite volunteers to name the four steps of shared leadership the author suggests we can find in the passage. List these on a large sheet of paper or a board. Invite participants to look again at the passage from Exodus and find where the text supports each of the steps named in the chapter. Discuss:

- Many Christians think that they hire a pastor to do the work of the church. What do you think?
- There obviously are benefits of shared leadership for the leader. Are there benefits for those with whom leadership is shared? Are there also benefits to the community as a whole?
- How is leadership carried out in our congregation? Do we embody an understanding of shared leadership? How are leaders nurtured and inspired? Are there aspects of leadership that could be strengthened? If so, what are they?

Examine the Role of Sacred Spaces   p. 134

Review the information in the text about the Tent of Meeting (sometimes called the Tabernacle). Have the group examine the diagram of the tabernacle and the illustration showing its central physical position in the midst of the Israelites. Ask volunteers to point out features of the tent and its furnishings. Discuss some of the following:

- The author compares the Tent of Meeting and its features with the portable thrones for Pharaoh in Egyptian temples. What parallels does he note? Why does he observe that the similarities should come as no surprise?

- He notes that the Tabernacle functioned as both palace and temple. What did these functions signify about the Holy One?
- There was a time in our history when the most beautiful and architecturally meaningful buildings were churches and other religious structures. Those structures were designed to be visible reminders of God's presence and to draw people into God's presence. Which structures in today's world provide the most meaningful and inspiring architecture? What, if anything, do you think this indicates about our culture and where we place our priorities?
- Some Christians are uncomfortable with making large expenditures on buildings, preferring to put their resources into mission and outreach. What do you think about this issue? How do you think congregations should decide what is appropriate to spend on a building?
- How does our church building function as a "thin place"? What are "thin places" in your world?
- The author asks: Did God really need a tent to dwell among the people? How do you respond?

Explore Grumbling in the Wilderness

A major theme running through Exodus and the Book of Numbers is the grumbling, criticizing, and complaining of the Israelites, with ten such passages found in the two books. Ask seven participants to read from Exodus 16 in round-robin fashion: Verses 1-4, 5-8, 9-12, 13-21, 22-26, 27-30, 31-36. Form pairs, and ask participants to discuss the following with their partner:

- Describe a time when you were criticized, either in your capacity as a leader or in some other setting such as in your family or in the workplace. How did you handle the criticism? How did you respond to those criticizing you? Did you listen to your critics? What did you learn from the experience?

- If the criticism was leveled at you as a leader, what was your vision for the way you were acting as a leader? If you were being criticized for some action you took in your family or the workplace, what vision was shaping the way you made the decision or interacted with your critics?
- When have you been the critic yourself? Was your criticism framed in constructive ways, or were you, like the Israelites, grumbling and complaining without offering suggestions for changing the situation?

In the large group, ask for a few observations or insights gleaned from the activity. Then ask:

- What is your vision of the "Promised Land"? What are some ways to keep that vision front and center when we are frustrated or discouraged by a situation?

Encounter the Paralysis of Fear

Invite volunteers to summarize what happened when after two years of wandering in the wilderness, the Israelites set up camp just a few miles from the Promised Land.

In previous sessions we examined the nature of fear—from Pharaoh's fear of the growing Hebrew population, to a different understanding of the word *fear*, to what it means to fear the Lord. So, considering these meanings of fear, ask participants to consider what they fear and why. Encourage them to list these fears in their journals. After allowing a few minutes for reflection and writing, ask them to pair off and discuss the following:

- Have you ever been paralyzed by fear about something? What was the situation? How did you overcome your fear?
- In what ways might fear prevent us from entering the "Promised Land" of a more fulfilling life?

In the large group, remind participants that in session 1, they explored the relationship of fear to courage and trust in God. Ask them to revisit the entries they made in their journals to the following:

- In my own life, I am fearful about _____.

- I will seek to respond with courage, despite my fear, to
  _____.

- A difficult or heartbreaking situation with which I am dealing
  is_____.

- I will seek to put my trust in God and in God's working
  through myself and others. I will commit to listening more
  fully for the Spirit's word by engaging in practices such as
  _____.

Ask:

- In light of what we've discussed in this session, would you
  respond differently to these open-ended statements now? Would
  you add to them?

Reflect on Ways to Respond to Wilderness Wanderings

In this session, wandering in the wilderness has been characterized as
a metaphor for times when a person is experiencing a difficult or painful
circumstance, or when uncertainty, fear, or doubt permeates one's life. But
wilderness experiences can also be shorthand for times when one is tested,
as Jesus was tested in the wilderness, or seeking clarity of call, as when John
the Baptist received God's call in the wilderness. In the early centuries of
Christianity, Christian hermits and ascetics called the Desert Fathers and
Mothers also dwelt in the desert wilderness.

Invite the group to call out, popcorn style, characteristics of a
metaphorical wilderness experience, such as silence or distance from other
people. Invite them to record these characteristics in their journals. Then
generate a list of possible spiritual practices they might explore in the
coming week that could, in some sense, replicate the wilderness experience
or wilderness wandering. This might include setting aside a time and place
away from others to meditate, walking a labyrinth, simply walking as a
spiritual exercise, or spending regular time praying for discernment about a
challenging circumstance in their lives.

Encourage them to commit to one of these practices in the coming
week.

More Activities (Optional)

Explore Other "Thin Places"

One function of beautiful architecture in religious buildings is to serve as a tangible reminder that God is with us. The author speaks of "thin spaces" where heaven and earth meet, noting for example that Jews still come and pray before the western foundation wall of the Temple believing that it is a "thin space."

Invite participants to think beyond beautiful buildings to other places where they have had profound experiences of God's presence. Call the group's attention to the three sheets of paper you prepared before the session. Invite them to reflect on where and when they have experienced a thin place in a physical location; where and when they have had what people often call a mountaintop experience; or where and when they have experienced God with them in a painful or difficult circumstance. Ask them to jot down that experience in a few words on the appropriate sheet.

After allowing a few minutes for participants to reflect and write, ask one or two volunteers to describe their experience. Then discuss:

- What does the author tell us was the function of the Tent of Meeting?
- In what ways does our church building remind us of God's presence?
- What are tangible reminders of other "thin place" experiences you have had?

Churches and synagogues are visible reminders of God's presence with us. With that in mind, the author suggests that as we pass a church, a synagogue, or another religious building, we might take a moment to pray and remember that God is with us. If participants can identify visible reminders of other "thin place" experiences, such as photos of a place or a person, they may want to display the reminder where they will see it often.

Walking in the Footsteps of Moses: Part 5

Invite participants to locate the Sinai Peninsula and use self-stick notes to mark the locations of Ramesses, Kadesh Barnea, Petra, and Hebron on the map or map sketch.

H. S. Palmer, who accompanied his explorer-brother, wrote of the Sinai, "It is a desert, certainly, in the fullest sense of the word, but a desert of rock, gravel, and boulder, of gaunt peaks, dreary ridges and arid valleys and plateaux, the whole forming a scene of stern desolation which fully merits its description as the 'great and terrible wilderness.'"* Invite participants to look at the photos of the Sinai Peninsula and examine the topographical map in the chapter.

Examine Examples of Grumbling

The author tells us that there are ten examples of the Israelites' complaining across two books of Scripture. Depending on the size of your group, assign one of the following to each of ten individuals, pairs, or small groups:

Exodus 14:10-12; 15:23-24; 16:2-3; 17:1-4; 32:1-10; Numbers 11:1-2, 4-6, 16-20; 12:1-3; 14:2-4.

Discuss:

- What was at the root of the grumbling?
- Do you ever complain to God? If so, what are your complaints?
- In the Israelites' complaints, what was the role of fear? of trust? What role do these two factors play in your own complaints to God?

Wrapping Up

Here is a list of the four lessons that Moses learned in the wilderness:

1. Ask for help, none of us can make it to the Promised Land alone.
2. Sacred spaces matter to God and are reminders of God's presence in our midst.
3. Grumbling, criticizing, and complaining are a part of life. Don't give up!
4. When you face the giants that make you afraid, trust God.

---

* W. F. Hume, *The Topography and Geology of the Peninsula of Sinai* Cairo: National Printing Department, 1906), 11.

These are lessons that he says Moses learned in the wilderness and that he suggests we must learn in our own wilderness wanderings. Ask participants to consider a past wilderness wandering experience, or one they can imagine affecting their life. Then ask them to name the lesson among the four that they would identify as potentially being:

- the most helpful;
- the greatest challenge.

Remind the group to read chapter 6 before the next session.

Closing Activity

Close by singing or reciting a hymn with images of wilderness wanderings and petitions for God's guidance: "Guide Me, O Thou Great Jehovah."

Closing Prayer

God of the covenant, we give thanks for your enduring presence in our lives. Help us to be aware that you are with us in our wilderness wanderings. Walk alongside us, both in our wanderings and as we seek to be ever closer to the Promised Land. In the name of Jesus we pray. Amen.

6.

DON'T FORGET...PASS IT ON

Planning the Session

Session Goals

As a result of conversations and activities connected with this session, group members should begin to:

- explore the emphasis in Deuteronomy on passing down the faith;
- examine loving God and loving neighbor in the Deuteronomy summaries;
- encounter the concept of seasons of faith and how they relate to faith life;
- reflect on a vision of the Promised Land.

Scriptural Foundation

[Then Moses said,] Israel, listen! Our God is the LORD! Only the LORD!

Love the LORD your God with all your heart, all your being, and all your strength. These words that I am commanding you today must always be on your minds. Recite them to your children.…

In the future, your children will ask you, "What is the meaning of the laws, the regulations, and the case laws that the LORD our God commanded you?" tell them: We were Pharaoh's slaves in Egypt. But the LORD brought us out of Egypt with a mighty hand."

(Deuteronomy 6:4-7, 20-21)

When you eat, get full, build nice houses, and settle down, and when your herds and your flocks are growing large, your silver and gold are multiplying, and everything you have is thriving, don't become arrogant, forgetting the LORD your God:

> the one who rescued you from Egypt, from the house of slavery.…

Don't think to yourself, My own strength and abilities have produced all this prosperity for me. Remember the LORD your God! He's the one who gives you the strength to be prosperous.

(Deuteronomy 8:12-14, 17-18)

Special Preparation

- Decide if you will do any of the optional activities. If you decide to view a segment of Martin Luther King Jr.'s sermon "I See the Promised Land" ("I've Been to the Mountaintop"), locate the clip on www.youtube.com and arrange for viewing it. If participants will read the entire text, download and print the sermon from www.americanrhetoric.com or plan to have them use their smartphones to read it.
- For the Love God/Love Neighbor reminders, you will need two sheets of posterboard and other art materials such as magazines, scissors, glue, and colored markers. If your group is large, get additional sheets of posterboard and plan for four working groups.
- For the activity about walking in Moses' footsteps, you will again need a large map or an outline sketch on large paper and self-stick notes (or index cards and tape).

Getting Started

Opening Activity

Welcome participants to this final session of the study. Gather together. Point out that as the chapter begins, Adam Hamilton invites us to think about the following:

- What would you want to say to your family and friends if you knew you were dying?

Allow a few minutes for participants to list in their journals some statements or affirmations they would include in a letter or video for those most important to them. Then ask volunteers to report one thing from their list, and print it on a large sheet of paper or a board. Invite others to add statements or affirmations not already on the list, and continue until everyone has had an opportunity to report.

Tell the group that in this final session, they will be exploring Moses' farewell discourses—his final sermons to the Israelites.

Opening Prayer

Pray together, using the following prayer or one of your own choosing.

God of the wilderness and of the Promised Land, we know that you will always be with us, even as two or three are gathered together. We give thanks that your presence is enduring. Grant that we may be ever more aware of that presence as we seek to encounter you more fully through Scripture. Amen

Learning Together

Video Study and Discussion

The Israelites don't trust God to protect them in the Promised Land, and so God decrees that they will stay in the desert for forty years. When the next generation arises, Moses leads them to Mount Nebo, where he bids them farewell and, with God's help, views the Promised Land before he dies.

- How do you think Moses felt when he realized he would never reach the Promised Land? If you were speaking with him about it, what would you say?
- What are some ways in which we can teach the next generation, "Don't forget…pass it on"?

Book and Bible Study and Discussion

Explore Passing on the Faith

Call the group's attention to what Adam Hamilton tells us about the Book of Deuteronomy, inviting them to name pertinent facts. List those facts on a board or a large sheet of paper. If any of the following are not named, add them to the list:

- Deuteronomy summarizes Israel's story and God's covenant with Israel;
- It is written as a series of sermons or addresses, making it both easier to follow and much shorter than the combined accounts of Exodus, Leviticus, and Numbers;
- Jesus quotes Deuteronomy more often than any other text in the Old Testament except the Psalms.

Call particular attention to what Hamilton identifies as a primary theme of the book: Moses' concern that the Israelites pass down the faith to their children. Invite a volunteer to read aloud Deuteronomy 6:6-7 and another volunteer to read aloud 6:22-25. Discuss some of the following:

- Hamilton tells us that faith, whether Israel's faith or ours, will always be just one generation away from extinction. What does he mean by this? Do you agree?
- He observes that while we may take our children to church, we sometimes fail to have meaningful, authentic conversations with them about what we really believe about God, how we've seen God work in our lives, and our experience of God in prayer or in worship. In your own experience, have you had these kinds of conversations with your children? What was the response?

- He suggests that grandparents may be the key to the future of the faith. If you are not a parent or a grandparent, what do you think your role is with the children and youth of our church?
- What do you think are the most effective ways of passing down the faith to the next generation?

Examine the Summaries of Torah

Hamilton's book includes two longer passages from Deuteronomy that in effect summarize the whole of Torah. Invite someone to read aloud Deuteronomy 10:12-22 and someone else to read Deuteronomy 11:13-21.

Ask a volunteer to read aloud Deuteronomy 6:4, the one commandment that Hamilton tells us stands above all the rest. He notes that faithful Jews hang this verse on the doorframes of their homes, reciting it every morning and every night and hoping to recite it once more before taking their last breath.

Ask a volunteer to continue reading Deuteronomy 6:5-9, and note that Jesus summarized the whole of the law similarly in Matthew 22:37-39—love God and love neighbor. Discuss:

- As Christians, we are not enjoined to place the verses from Deuteronomy on our doorframes. But the Great Commandment as Jesus articulated it is central to who we are as disciples of Christ. What might be some ways to keep the commandment front and center in our minds?

Encounter Seasons of Faith

Call attention to the diagram included in the chapter. Invite a volunteer to explain Old Testament scholar Walter Brueggemann's explanation of the seasons of life—what he identifies as the seasons of orientation, disorientation, and reorientation that Israel seemed to cycle through regularly.

Ask another volunteer to describe the way Hamilton uses the seasons to describe the story of the Israelites' journey out of Egypt, through the wilderness, and to the brink of the Promised Land.

Invite participants to think about their own faith life. Ask them to print the three seasons of orientation, disorientation, and reorientation in their journals and to think about a time when their faith life could be described using those terms. Ask them to reflect in writing on that time.

If there are group members who have trouble identifying such a time, invite them to reflect in silence as others write, and encourage them to continue reflection in the coming days.

Reflect on a Vision of the Promised Land

Invite someone to read aloud Deuteronomy 34:1-4 (also included in the book chapter). Though Moses was not allowed to enter the Promised Land, the Lord did allow him to see it. The author imagines Moses on a mountaintop viewing the entirety of the land, even that part which would have been physically impossible to see.

Hamilton notes that the Promised Land is an ideal, a place where God's will is done, a taste of heaven on earth—what Jesus called the Kingdom of God. Invite participants to respond in their journals to the following questions he poses:

- What is your Promised Land?
- What is the compelling and overarching vision to which you'll devote your life?

More Activities (Optional)

Create Love God / Love Neighbor Reminders

Invite participants to learn more about the Shema, the prayer that Jews are to recite each morning and evening. Participants can use their smartphones to access information at the website Judaism 101. Point out that while Hamilton focuses on Deuteronomy 6:4-9, Jews also include Deuteronomy 11:13-21 as well as Numbers 15:37-41.

For Christians, the words of the Great Commandment—to love God with all your heart and soul and mind, and your neighbor as yourself—summarize what it means to be a disciple.

Form two smaller groups. Assign "Love God" to one smaller group and "Love Neighbor" to the other. (In a very large class, form four smaller groups and have two of them work on each commandment.) Give each smaller group a sheet of posterboard as well as other art materials. Ask them to put the words "Love God" or "Love Neighbor" in large letters in the center, then glue pictures or words cut from magazines or print words or symbols on the remainder of the posterboard to depict what is entailed in each commandment.

When the smaller groups have finished working, ask each one to explain their creation to the large group. Display the creations in your space. Participants may want to take a picture of each creation with their smartphones and save the photos as a daily reminder.

See a Sermon of Martin Luther King Jr.

Invite the group to view the culmination of Martin Luther King Jr.'s sermon, "I See the Promised Land" ("I've Been to the Mountaintop"), delivered at the Mason Temple Church of God the night before he was assassinated. If time allows, participants could read the entire sermon. Discuss:

- Dr. King refers to the Promised Land. How do you think he would have described the Promised Land, given the realities of 1968 in Memphis and in many other cities across the land?
- In practical terms, how might Dr. King have described what it means to love God and to love the neighbor as yourself?

Walking in the Footsteps of Moses: Part 6

As in the previous five sessions, ask participants to refer to the information in chapter 6 in which the author refers to his travels in Egypt as he sought to walk in Moses' footsteps. Ask them to identify significant landmarks or locations, such as Edom, Moab, the King's Highway, Mount Nebo, and Jericho, and record each name on a self-stick note. Place the notes at the appropriate location on the map (or on your sketch). Also ask them to examine the photographs in the chapter.

Wrapping Up

In the introduction to the study, Adam Hamilton tells us that his purpose in writing this book was not to write a biography, nor to write a verse-by-verse exposition, nor to add another scholarly commentary to the many already available. Instead, he hoped to help readers not only come to know Moses, but to see how his life and story speak to our lives and stories today. In Hamilton's view, Moses' story reveals something to us about God, about ourselves, and about God's will for our lives.

Ask participants to quickly thumb through the chapters. Invite them to name insights that have been revealed to them during the course of the study.

Closing Activity

Recall that in the opening activity, participants imagined what they would tell family and friends if they were dying. Ask them now to consider the following:

- What would you say to friends and family about your life of faith? What aspects of your faith would you want to pass on?

Invite all to respond briefly. Then remind the group that Moses, and people of faith today, are concerned that we will always be only one generation away from the extinction of our faith. Invite participants to reflect on what they just affirmed about their faith. If they have not already done so, encourage them to pass on their faith story to family and friends.

Sing or recite together the hymn "Come, Thou Fount of Every Blessing."

Closing Prayer

Open our hearts, O God of grace, to the importance of passing on this faith we treasure. Grant us the eloquence to speak of your love and the commitment to make those words real in our actions. For we ask it in the name of Jesus Christ, in whose life your abiding love was made real. Amen.